By Robin Twiddy

BookLife PUBLISHING

©2019
BookLife Publishing Ltd.
King's Lynn
Norfolk PE30 4LS

ISBN: 978-1-78637-550-6

Written by:
Robin Twiddy

Edited by:
Emilie Dufresne

Designed by:
Danielle Jones

All rights reserved
Printed in Malaysia

A catalogue record for this book is available from the British Library.

All facts, statistics, web addresses and URLs in this book were verified as valid and accurate at time of writing. No responsibility for any changes to external websites or references can be accepted by either the author or publisher.

OXFORDSHIRE LIBRARY SERVICE	
3303473442	
Askews & Holts	04-Apr-2019
J948.022	£12.99

IMAGE CREDITS

Cover & throughout - HappyPictures, Anna Panova, Roxiller13, Vasif Maharov, Vialas, Oceloti, Radiocat. 4 - DenisKrivoy. 5 - Alex Gontar, GraphicsRF, NirdalArt. 7 - NataliaMalc, ArtMari, MoreVector, billedfab. 10 - ArtShotPhoto. 11 - alexmstudio. 13 - perori. 17 - AkimD. 19 - tykcartoon. 20 - HappyPictures. 22 - Vector Tradition. Images are courtesy of Shutterstock.com. With thanks to Getty Images, Thinkstock Photo and iStockphoto.

CONTENTS

Page 4   Planning a Raid
Page 6   Weapons
Page 8   Axes
Page 10 Spears
Page 12 Swords
Page 14 Armour
Page 16 Shields
Page 18 Our Greatest Weapon
Page 20 The Longboat
Page 22 Britain, Here We Come!
Page 24 Glossary and Index

Words that look like THIS can be found in the glossary on page 24.

PLANNING a RAID

Hi! My name is Arvid and I am a Viking. The jarl (say: yarl), who is our leader, is organising a raid. He says that there are lots of riches in a land across the sea — they call it Britain!

A successful raid of Britain will bring us lots of HONOUR and RESPECT from other Vikings!

A raid is when we sail our ships and fighters to another land without them knowing. If the people there are clever, they will pay us <u>TRIBUTE</u> — where they give us what we want. If they are not clever, we will take their gold and silver by fighting them.

SCANDINAVIA
(We Vikings live here.)

BRITAIN

WEAPONS

We will need lots of weapons if we are going to have a successful raid. Every free Viking man carries a weapon — you might have to defend your honour in a <u>DUEL</u> at any time!

In Viking <u>CULTURE</u>, honour is more important than <u>POSSESSIONS</u>.

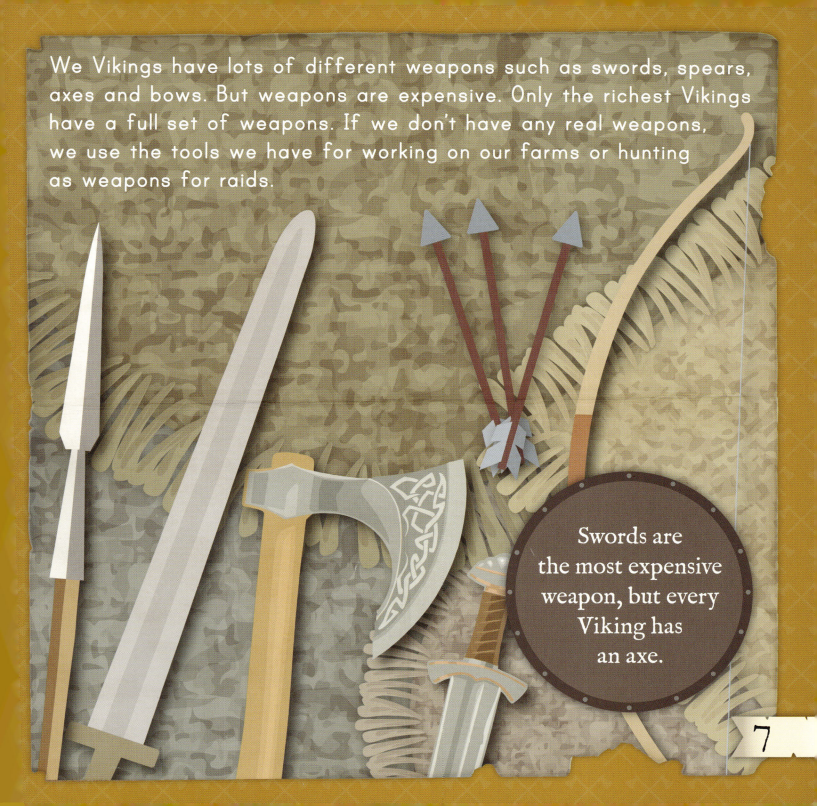

We Vikings have lots of different weapons such as swords, spears, axes and bows. But weapons are expensive. Only the richest Vikings have a full set of weapons. If we don't have any real weapons, we use the tools we have for working on our farms or hunting as weapons for raids.

Swords are the most expensive weapon, but every Viking has an axe.

AXES

Axes are great weapons. We have small hand axes like this one. You can hold two — one in each hand, which will do lots of damage. Or, you could just hold one, and hold a shield in the other hand. Shields are great for protecting you in deadly situations!

This is a bearded axe. It has a hook at the bottom of the blade to pull an enemy's shield away from them.

We also use two-handed axes. These are really long, but it is important that they aren't too heavy, so that they are easy to swing. Two-handed axes are good for reaching enemies behind their shields.

This is a great weapon to use to keep yourself a good distance from your enemies.

SPEARS

A lot of the warriors going on the raid will take spears. These are a lot cheaper to make than swords. A spear can be thrown or used to poke and jab. I've even seen skilled warriors catch a spear in the air and throw it back at the enemy!

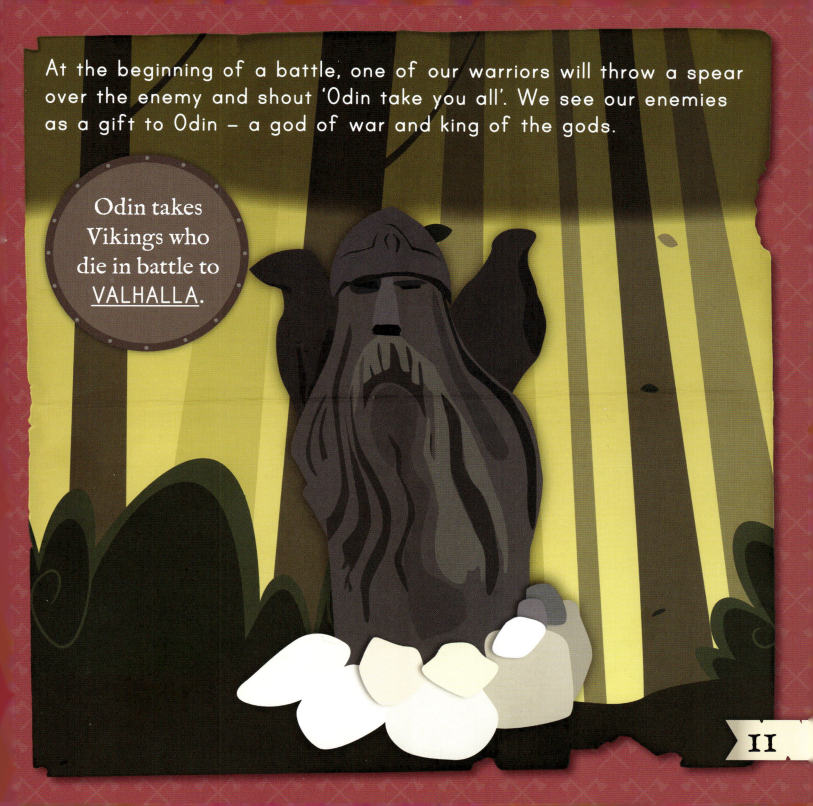

At the beginning of a battle, one of our warriors will throw a spear over the enemy and shout 'Odin take you all'. We see our enemies as a gift to Odin – a god of war and king of the gods.

Odin takes Vikings who die in battle to <u>VALHALLA</u>.

SWORDS

Swords are, of course, excellent weapons. But you won't see many of them on a Viking raid. They are so expensive to make that, if you see one, it probably belongs to a jarl, or one of his bodyguards.

I have a sword, even though I am not a jarl or a bodyguard. Do you want to see it?

If you are lucky enough to have a sword, like me, then it might have been handed down to you by your father as an HEIRLOOM, like mine was. Viking swords are used with one hand and have blades on both edges. They can be beautifully decorated with ENGRAVINGS and patterns.

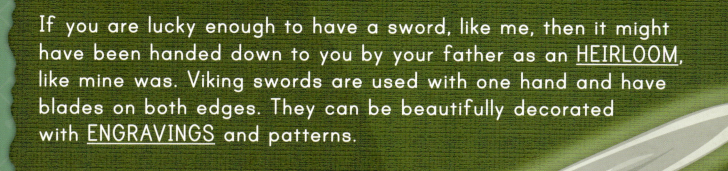

Most Viking swords have names. This one is called Leg-Biter.

ARMOUR

There are three main types of armour you might see on a Viking. These are: helmets, chain mail and leather armour. If you have lots of money, you might have all of these...

HELMET

LEATHER VEST

CHAIN MAIL

Chain mail is made from lots of tiny metal rings linked together. It is really hard to make, but it is the best kind of armour we have. Some Vikings have helmets, and they are basically just bowls to put on your head. Some have a nose guard.

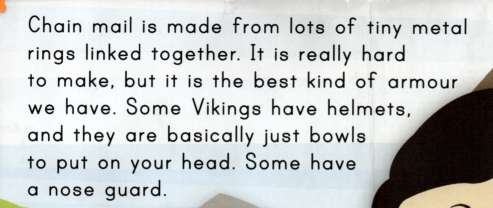

Maybe I should put some horns on this? No, that would look silly. We don't need horns - real Vikings wouldn't do that.

SHIELDS

Every Viking has a shield. Our shields are round, and about 80 centimetres in <u>DIAMETER</u>. They are made of wood and have a hand grip in the middle. We sometimes cover the front of the shield in leather to help protect it.

Shields are so important that we have laws about how they are built – and trust me, you don't want to break a Viking law!

Our shields aren't just for protection. They work well as weapons too. Having that handle in the middle means you can spin and turn them easily. Never UNDERESTIMATE a Viking with just a shield. They can cause some serious damage.

Shields have leather straps - this is so we can carry them on our backs when we aren't fighting.

OUR Greatest WEAPON

Those Britons had better watch out, because we have a secret weapon – Odin's favourite warriors, the berserkers. Even normal Vikings think these guys are fierce! Berserkers wear the skins of bears and wolves and believe that, when they fight, they are POSSESSED by the spirits of those animals.

Berserkers are fearless on the battlefield. When we attack, the berserkers usually lead the charge. We try to keep away from them during a battle because they can go into a blind rage. This means they can attack the enemy, each other and even trees and rocks.

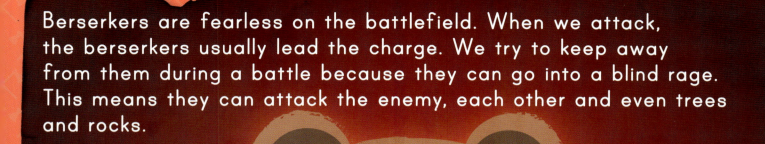

You will often see a berserker biting his shield before battle.

The LONGBOAT

This is the boat that is going to get us to Britain, and most importantly let us sneak up on the Britons through their rivers. Viking longboats are the fastest around. They have a sail but can also be rowed using oars if there is no wind.

Longboats can carry between 10 and 100 Vikings depending on how big they are.

20

Longboats don't have any beds so we will all sleep on the main deck. The front of the ship has a carving of a dragon or a snake. This will scare off the unfriendly spirits in other lands. The ships are so light that we can pick them up and carry them onto shore.

With this speedy longboat, we will be at their doors before they even see us coming!

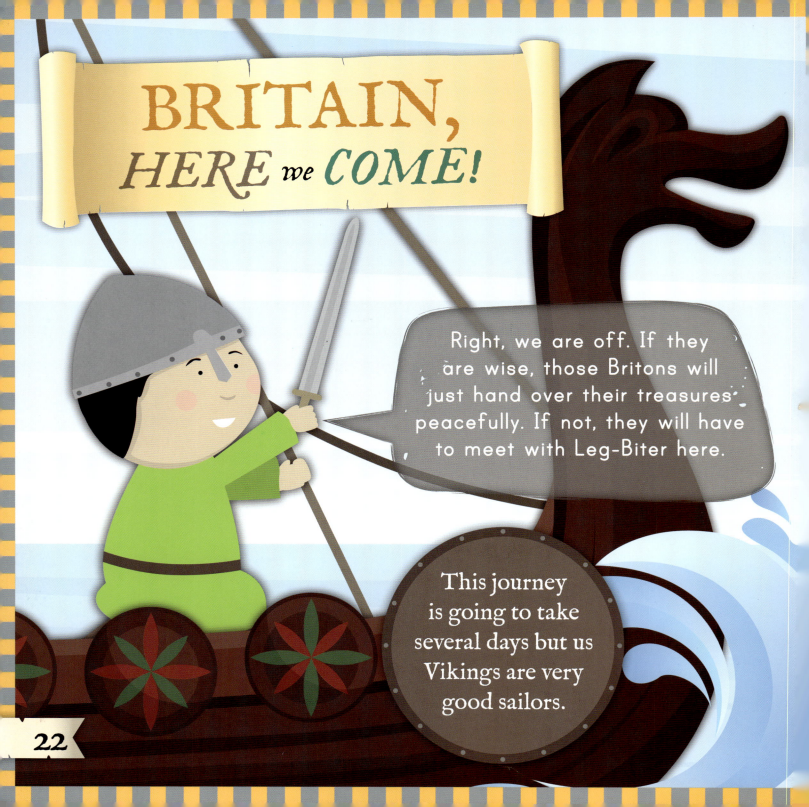

GLOSSARY

culture	the way of life and traditions of a group of people
diameter	the distance through the centre of an object
duel	an arranged fight involving two people
engravings	cuts or carvings made onto the surface of an object
heirloom	something passed down through a family
honour	when lots of people have respect for a person and their actions
monasteries	religious buildings that are home to monks or nuns
possessed	controlled or taken over by a spirit
possessions	physical things that someone owns
respect	feeling that something or someone is important
tribute	an act or gift meant to show respect
underestimate	to think something is less than it actually is
Valhalla	in Norse mythology, the hall of the dead where great heroes go after death

INDEX

berserkers 18–19
Britain 4–5, 20, 23
chain mail 14–15
enemies 8–11, 19
gold 5, 23
helmets 14–15
honour 4, 6
jarls 4, 12
leather 14, 16–17
longboats 20–21
monasteries 23
Odin 11, 18
respect 4
tribute 5
Valhalla 11